A Special Partnership

A practical guide for Named Persons and parents of children with special educational needs.

Prepared by

Linda Kerr (Information Officer, ENABLE)

Liz Sutherland (Special Needs Development Officer, Children in Scotland)

Joyce Wilson (Assistant Director, Sense Scotland)

© Crown Copyright 1994
First Published 1994

Applications for reproduction should be made to HMSO

British Library Cataloguing in Publication Data
A catalogue for this book is available from the British Library

ISBN 0 11 495237 X

HMSO publications are available from:

HMSO Bookshops
71 Lothian Road, Edinburgh, EH3 9AZ (0131) 228 4181
49 High Holborn, London, WC1V 6HB (0171) 873 0011
(Counter service only)
258 Broad Street, Birmingham, B1 2HE (0121) 643 3740
Southey House, 33 Wine Street, Bristol, BS1 2BQ (0117) 926 4306
9-21 Princess Street, Manchester, M60 8AS (0161) 834 7201
16 Arthur Street, Belfast, BT1 4GD (01232) 238451

HMSO Publications Centre
(Mail and telephone orders only)
PO Box 276, London, SW8 5DT
Telephone orders (0171) 873 9090
General enquiries (0171) 873 0011
(queuing system in operation for both numbers)

Contents

Preface

During the last decade, there has been a very significant and welcome change in our approach to the education of children and young people who, owing to some learning or other difficulty, such as physical disability, need help or support with their education beyond that which is normally provided.

At a recent national conference bringing together parents and professionals in this field, there was a clear consensus for greater understanding, greater cooperation and better consultation in making the key decisions affecting these children; there was a call for the breakdown of barriers between parents and professionals and for the improvement of links and communication between different professional groups.

As the parent of a child with special needs I particularly welcome the increased recognition given to the role of parents as the anchor, the keystone in a child's life. Some years ago, I remember an eminent paediatrician telling me that *parents know their children better than anyone else*. It is so important to recognise and believe this because, no matter how familiar we are as parents with the system, we frequently find it hard to cope. We may feel isolated and threatened. How often have I heard mothers and fathers comment that dealing with the professionals is harder than dealing with their own child.

The law gives parents the right to turn to a Named Person for advice and information. The Named Person's role is to support the parent as a friend, ally and advocate. The Named Person can greatly contribute towards ensuring the successful development of an equal partnership between parents and professionals. It was in recognition of parents' need to be supported through what can be confusing and stressful times, that Lady Mary Warnock, reporting to the committee of enquiry into the education of handicapped children and young people in 1978, first put forward the concept of Named Persons.

This guide has been prepared to provide parents and Named Persons with practical suggestions for ways of becoming more involved as equal partners with professionals in supporting their children's education. It will not answer all the questions parents and Named Persons may have about special educational needs, but it will answer some of them.

I hope that parents and professionals alike will find the guide useful. At times of change – and we will as parents see significant change in the next few years in the way education and other services are delivered – good information is particularly important. Information leads to empowerment, and we owe it to all our children to ensure that what is theirs as a right is turned into a reality.

Barbara Kelly CBE

Acknowledgements

The writers of this guide are grateful to the many individuals and organisations who provided helpful and detailed comments on the drafts of the text. In particular they would like to thank all the parents and Named Persons who gave help and advice.

Thanks are also due to Professor Sheila Wolfendale, Department of Psychology, University of East London, for permission to include her guidelines about the contribution which parents can make to their child's assessment.

Financial assistance from the Scottish Office Education Department towards the overall costs of producing this guide is also gratefully acknowledged.

And finally, thanks too, to the secretarial staff who supported this project, especially Lynn Whigham, Children in Scotland.

The Authors

Liz Sutherland has worked in the field of special needs in the UK for 17 years, holding posts with Children in Scotland's Special Needs Forum, LEAD (Scotland) and Edinburgh University's CALL Centre. Joyce Wilson has worked in the voluntary sector in Scotland since 1984 and is currently Depute Director of Sense Scotland, an organisation working with deafblind people and people with multiple sensory impairments. Linda Kerr has been Information Officer with ENABLE, the largest voluntary organisation in Scotland concerned with the needs of people with learning disabilities and their families, since 1985.

Introduction

This guide has been written for parents and Named Persons. It gives practical advice, suggestions and information to enable them to work together effectively with practitioners.

Other people who might find this guide helpful include teachers, psychologists, therapists, advisers, health visitors, child care workers, community paediatricians, social workers, staff of voluntary organisations, other parents and family members – anyone concerned with children with special educational needs.

This guide is not an authoritative guide to the law and should not be read as such. It is merely intended to be an introduction. For more detailed information readers are advised to consult the reading material listed in Chapter 9, especially the HMSO/Scottish Consumer Council publication *In special need* (1989) and the Scottish Office Education Department publication *A parents' guide to special educational needs.*

The first time a significant word appears in the text it is printed in bold type. An explanation of these terms is given in Chapter 10.

Chapter 1

Special Educational Needs and Named Persons

Parents who have a child with **special educational needs** may need all kinds of information and support. This guide looks at how parents can become involved in their child's education and describes one particular source of support – the **Named Person.**

Named Persons are appointed by the education authority to advise and assist parents. They were introduced by legislation which came into force in 1983 along with the term "special educational needs".

If a school cannot meet a child's educational needs from its own normal resources, special provision may be required and the child is described as having "special educational needs". If the child's educational needs are so "pronounced, specific or complex" that they "require continuing **review**" then the education authority is required to open a **Record of Needs** for that child.

The decision to open a Record of Needs is taken after a thorough **assessment** of the child's needs has been made. The Record includes a description of the **learning difficulty,** the child's special educational needs, and what services will be provided to meet that child's needs. The Record is a legal document and the procedures involved in opening it can be complex. Here parents may well find they need advice, information and support.

If a child is going to be assessed for a Record parents will be given the name of an **officer of the education authority** who can answer parents' queries. In most areas this person will be the local **educational psychologist,** although in some areas it is a member of the education directorate of the authority.

> The Named Person should not be confused with the officer of the education authority available to give advice and information *before* a recording decision is reached (and afterwards if necessary). This officer acts on behalf of the **education authority.** The Named Person, appointed after consultation with parents, supports and acts on behalf of parents.

Not all children with special educational needs will have a Record of Needs and, with or without a Record, children can expect to receive an education which meets their needs. The policy and practice of recording varies from region to region. In parts of Scotland, there are some children with special educational needs in special schools who do not have Records of Needs. There are also some children in mainstream schools who do have Records. 1.2% of *all* school pupils have a Record of Needs (SOED Statistical Bulletin, *Provision of education for pupils with special educational needs,* 1994). Recent research in this area – Thomson, Riddell, Dyer (1989) – provides more details.

If, as a result of assessment, the education authority decides to open a Record, then parents will be invited by the authority to nominate a Named Person. The Named

Person's role is to support the parents and to act on their behalf if asked to do so.

There is no obligation to have a Named Person and some parents prefer not to have one. However, there is no doubt that, potentially, the Named Person can provide good support to parents. This guide promotes the role of the Named Person and makes suggestions for the positive development of this role.

Chapter 2

Identifying, Assessing and Reviewing Special Educational Needs

Education authorities have the power to identify children with special educational needs at the earliest possible age, and are under a duty, if it is possible, to do so from the age of two. (They are also obliged to assess children under the age of two who appear to have special educational needs if the child's parents make that request, unless they feel the request is unreasonable.)

Parents who think that their child is having some difficulties can approach the education authority for advice. The authority may wish to carry out a full assessment, possibly with a view to opening a Record of Needs. Children younger than two may already have been identified through health or other community services and links already established with the education authority. Health visitors, GPs, or staff at any pre-school facility can ask the education authority for an assessment or can be approached by parents for advice.

Assessment involves finding out more about the child, his or her abilities and difficulties. Assessments for Records of Needs are generally arranged by an educational psychologist employed by the local authority education department. They involve a range of other professional staff like teachers and sometimes therapists. A formal medical examination is also necessary.

Contributing to assessments

Parents are the people who know most about their child. Their experience and understanding is invaluable and needs to be shared with key workers. Education authorities around Scotland have different ways of involving parents in assessment. A meeting, or series of meetings, will usually be held to discuss the child's needs.

Parents can expect:
- to be invited to participate in such meetings
- to be given ample notice of them
- to be encouraged to make their own contribution to them
- to have their contribution regarded as valuable.

Some authorities have written information about the arrangements they make for special education including recording procedures which should be available to parents. Every education authority has a duty to disseminate information about the arrangements they make to assess children with special educational needs. The Scottish Office Education Department produces a free guide for parents – *A parents' guide to special educational needs* – which is available either directly from the SOED or locally through education authorities.

If the question of opening a Record is being considered parents can also expect to be given the name of the officer of the education authority who will answer initial queries.

Parents will be asked to give their views on their child's needs and the measures they think are required to meet those needs. One practical idea might be for parents to draw up a written profile of their child's abilities and difficulties. An outline of what the profile might include is given below. Named Persons might be able to help parents with this. As far as possible and appropriate, parents should encourage children to contribute their own views, too.

If the education authority then decides to open a Record of Needs, one thing that will happen is that parents will be asked formally to prepare a written description of their views on their child's needs. This description will then go into part 7 of the Record. The early exercise of writing a profile of a child's needs could be a useful first step towards this and again Named Persons could be helpful at this stage.

If the decision is *not* to open a Record parents could ask for a note of everyone's contribution to the assessment and share this with key individuals like the child's teacher. At this point they will be given information by the education authority about their rights to appeal and they may wish to seek further advice. (See *In special need*, Scottish Consumer Council (HMSO, 1989) for detailed information about appeals procedures).

Guidelines for parents' contributions to their child's statutory assessment

These guidelines are to help you with your contributions to the assessment. You do not have to use them if you do not want to. You may change the order, leave bits out or add things you may feel to be important. Your written contribution may be as short or as long as you wish.

A – The early years

1. What do you remember about the early years that might help?

2. What was your child like as a young baby?

3. Were you happy about progress at the time?

4. When did you first feel things were not right?

5. What happened?

6. What advice or help did you receive – from whom?

B – What is your child like now

1. **General health** – Eating and sleeping habits; general fitness, absences from school, minor ailments – coughs and colds. Serious illnesses/accidents – periods in hospital. Any medicine or special diet? General alertness – tiredness, signs of use of drugs – smoking, drinking, glue–sniffing.

2. **Physical skills** – Walking, running, climbing – riding a bike, football or other games, drawing pictures, writing, doing jigsaws; using construction kits, household gadgets, tools, sewing.

3. **Self help** – Level of personal independence – dressing, etc; making bed, washing clothes, keeping room tidy, coping with day to day routine; budgeting pocket money, general independence – getting out and about.

4. **Communication** – Level of speech, explains, describes events, people, conveys information (eg. messages to and from school), joins in conversations; uses telephone.

5. **Playing and learning at home** – How your child spends time, watching TV, reading for pleasure and information, hobbies, concentration, sharing.

6. **Activities outside** – Belonging to clubs, sporting activities, happy to go alone.

7. **Relationships** – With parents, brothers and sisters; with friends; with other adults (friends and relations) at home generally, 'outside' generally.

8. **Behaviour at home** – Co-operates, shares, listens to and carries out requests, helps in the house, offers help, fits in with family routine and 'rules'. Moods good and bad, sulking – temper tantrums; demonstrative, affectionate.

9. **At school** – Relationships with other children and teachers; progress with reading, writing, number, other subjects and activities at school. How the school has helped/not helped with your child. Have you been asked to help with school work – hearing child read – with what result?

Does your child enjoy school?

What does your child find easy or difficult?

C – Your general views

1. What do you think your child's special educational needs are?

2. How do you think these can be best provided for?

3. How do you compare your child with others of the same age?

4. What is your child good at or what does he or she enjoy doing?

5. What does your child worry about – is your child aware of difficulties?

6. What are your worries, concerns?

7. Is there any other information you would like to give
   a) about the family – major events that might have affected your child?
   b) reports from other people?

8. With whom would you like more contact?

9. How do you think your child's needs affect the needs of the family as a whole?

With thanks to
Professor Sheila Wolfendale
Department of Psychology, University of London

Assessment and review

Assessment is a continuous process. The progress of very young children especially needs to be regularly reviewed. Reviews of a child's educational progress will be carried out at various points throughout the child's school life, both formally and informally. Parents (and Named Persons) should feel they are just as much involved in these formal and informal review processes as in the early initial assessment. A child with a Record of Needs should have his or her needs reviewed regularly. Parents can request a review if there has not been one in the previous 12 months. When the child nears school leaving age (usually around 14¹) a first **Future Needs Assessment** meeting will be held (see Chapter 6).

Some authorities now have guidelines for parents on the conduct of formal reviews and Future Needs Assessments. For more information about assessment and reviews, see *In special need,* Scottish Consumer Council (HMSO, 1989).

Observations on the Recording process

Sometimes parents and education authority staff will disagree about the best way to meet a child's needs.

The term "special educational needs" can cover a broad range of abilities. For some children it will be clear that their needs are sufficiently complex to merit the opening of a Record of Needs. But for other children, especially those who do not have an identified condition, but who are clearly having problems with their learning, it may not be so straightforward. Some parents have said that their wish to have a Record opened in such circumstances has led them into conflict with the education authority.

The education authority has a duty both to assess a child's needs and then to provide appropriate services. However the education authority's budget is limited. Parents sometimes feel that there will not be enough money to meet all of a child's needs fully, and that the Record of Needs will merely state what can be afforded rather than everything the child needs. Sometimes, too, parents and professionals can disagree about whether the child's needs are complex enough to require continuing review.

When conflict or problems do arise it can be helpful for parents to have a supporter like the Named Person to turn to for help and advice. Education authorities have to demonstrate the efficient use of resources when making provision to meet children's special educational needs. It is essential therefore that parents provide the clearest possible views and supporting evidence about their child's needs and about any provision which they feel their child requires. The Named Person can play an invaluable role in helping parents to prepare such information and to ensure that all relevant people in the child's life are involved as appropriate.

These observations do not mean that the Recording process is always problematic. Clear, honest and sensitive communication between education authorities and parents will go a long way to prevent problems arising. Nor should the Named Person simply be thought of as someone to be brought in at times of crisis. The Named Person has a valuable role to play supporting parents – if parents wish it – at all stages in the assessment and review of a child's progress.

Chapter 3

The Named Person

Once a Record of Needs is opened for a child with special educational needs, parents will be invited by the education authority to discuss the appointment of someone (a Named Person), if they wish, whom they can approach for information and advice. The parent may choose *not* to have a Named Person. Where the child is aged 16 or over and capable of expressing a view, he or she has these rights instead of the parent. The name and address of the Named Person will be entered into the Record of Needs.

What does the Named Person do?

The Named Person is there to support parents. He or she should be someone whom parents can trust. The Named Person's role is to help parents express their views most effectively in matters to do with their child's education and to give advice. The appointment is usually seen as a long-term commitment, possibly for as long as the child will remain at school. Some parents however may prefer a shorter-term arrangement. It is possible to change the Named Person during a child's education.

When is the Named Person appointed?

Officially the Named Person is not appointed until the wording of the Record of Needs is agreed. This is during the final stage of the child's assessment. However some education authorities recognise that it is in the early stages of the process that parents often need most help. New draft guidance for local authorities on assessment and recording was issued by the Scottish Office Education Department in January 1994, and it recommends the earlier appointment of Named Persons in future. In the meantime there is nothing to stop parents seeking support and advice, or taking someone to meetings with them, during the initial stages of assessment and recording. The person who supports parents in this way may then go on to become their official Named Person.

How is the Named Person appointed?

It is very helpful if parents contact the person they would like to be appointed before discussing their choice with the education authority. After the parents have selected their Named Person, the education authority will write to the chosen person, appointing him or her officially as Named Person and giving information about the role of the Named Person. If they prefer, parents can ask the education authority to help them make the first approach to a possible Named Person. (It should be pointed out that the education authority need not accept a parent's nomination.)

What limitations are placed on the role of the Named Person?

A Named Person is someone who can be approached by parents for advice and support. He or she does not have a legally defined role. But, the very flexibility of the role can be an advantage – Named Persons are there to support parents in *any* way the parents want. A Named Person who is never approached by parents could end up doing nothing.

Keeping the Named Person informed

It is important for parents and Named Persons to clarify with the education authority what information will be passed on to Named Persons and by whom. Named Persons should not assume that the education authority will automatically tell them about dates of meetings, or send copies of relevant letters or reports. They have no legal entitlement here though good practice would encourage the building of mutual trust and respect between professionals, parents and Named Persons right from the start.

The role played by Named Persons will depend on the parent they represent, the needs of the child, the Named Person's skills and experience and the situation in which they find themselves. Some may wish to take a more active role than others. Here are some examples of how Named Persons can help.

The Named Person can:

- listen to parents and encourage them to be confident in expressing their views

- help parents to draw up a profile of their child (see Chapter 2)

- make telephone calls on behalf of parents

- accompany parents on visits to schools, especially the first visit

- sit in on meetings, ask the questions that are "difficult"

- listen at meetings, take notes and then discuss with parents what was said

- give a second opinion

- offer constructive criticism

- help parents to understand the assessment process, the roles of the various professionals, jargon etc.

- get information from other agencies

- accompany parents to appeal hearings (though not necessarily acting as their legal representative)

- keep records of meetings and correspondence

- help to write letters to officials

- help to fill in forms

- explain official documents, including the Record of Needs.

Chapter 4

Choosing a Named Person

. . . think and choose carefully. It has to be somebody you can trust, somebody that knows your child well and who can give you advice and help in making future decisions.   A parent

If parents do want the support of a Named Person the following guidelines may help in making a choice.

Who should be chosen as a Named Person?

No formal qualifications are necessary in order to become a Named Person. Anyone can act in this capacity. The most important qualification is that parents have confidence in their Named Person and feel they can turn to him or her for support.

Sometimes, expertise in a particular area (eg communication problems) can help. It can be especially useful if the Named Person has some understanding of the education system but expertise in education is not essential.

People who have carried out this role in the past have included the family minister, social workers, local chemists, family GPs, health visitors, family friends, neighbours, **pre-school home visiting teachers** (sometimes known as **educational visitors**), representatives from **voluntary organisations,** other parents – anyone in fact.

It is always helpful to consider what other commitments and responsibilities someone has before asking him or her to be a Named Person. A good choice will be someone who has enough time to be effective and whose other responsibilities do not conflict with the interests of the child and the family. Some parents have said that, in their experience, having the head teacher or the child's educational psychologist as a Named Person has not been helpful.

What makes a good Named Person?

Here are some qualities to look for when choosing a Named Person. Parents will need to decide which qualities are most important according to their own needs. If parents feel at ease in approaching someone to be their Named Person it is likely that a good choice has been made.

The Named Person is someone who:

• can be trusted and relied upon

• will respect confidentiality

• is a good listener

• is a good communicator

- will say if they disagree with parents

- can be easily contacted

- will probably be around for several years

- knows the parents and the child well

- knows the education system or is willing to find out about it

- has some free time

- is good at seeing things through

- has no potential conflict of interest

- ideally, is willing to make a long term commitment.

Can the Named Person be changed?

Parents can ask at any time to change their Named Person. The Named Person may move away or parents may later decide they had made the wrong choice. As the child grows older his or her needs may change and a Named Person with a different set of skills may be needed. If so, parents can simply write to the education authority and inform them of this decision. However, they should bear in mind that it is the education authority which officially appoints the Named Person and they may not accept the parents' choice.

How many Named Persons can parents have?

The Education (Scotland) Act 1980 refers to a single person and only one name can be inserted on the Record of Needs. However, depending on the particular needs of the child, a situation may arise where both the Named Person and parents would feel more confident if they could call on the support of someone who has particular experience and understanding. Parents and Named Persons should feel free to do this. If they then would like to involve this additional person in the formal process of recording, they should ask the education authority staff about the best way of doing this.

Even though parents have a Named Person they can continue to seek out other informal sources of advice at any time.

What if there are difficulties finding a suitable Named Person?

Sometimes parents will be unable to find a suitable person to act as their Named Person. If they feel unable to make their own choice, or uncomfortable with the person suggested by the education authority, it may be important to talk to others – friends, family, other parents, professionals, voluntary agencies – about this difficulty.

In the end parents may choose not to have a Named Person. This does not mean that parents cannot choose to have a Named Person at any time in future.

Chapter 5

The Named Person in Action

There are many ways in which parents and Named Persons may work together. The following examples show different ways parents and Named Persons can act in partnership.

Using counselling skills

Jean's mother and father disagree about the advantages and disadvantages of two schools suggested for her. Their Named Person, a neighbour and long-time friend, helps them to look objectively at what each school could offer. This enables Jean's parents to reach a decision about which they are both happy.

Liaising with other agencies

Chan's mother and father separate and he and his mother have to move house very quickly. They wish to move near his grandparents who live in another region. A neighbour and friend currently acts as Named Person but does not feel able to continue. Chan has been using the services of a national voluntary agency since he was born. One of the agency's staff is able to act as a transitional Named Person and to organise liaison with the new education authority, educational psychologist, housing and **social work departments. Case conferences** are held, a school chosen and housing arranged before the family moves and Chan starts his new school.

Representing the pupil's interests at Future Needs Assessments

Sharon is fourteen and has a severe communication impairment. She has gained communication skills through a great deal of hard and close work with teachers at her current school. Arrangements for post-school services are to be discussed at a Future Needs Assessment meeting. Several options will be considered. A friend of the family who teaches at another school and knows Sharon well has been Sharon's Named Person for ten years. He and her father discuss with Sharon how to ensure that Sharon's communication abilities will be supported through to any new placement. Sharon will not leave school for at least two years but they would all like to make sure there is enough forward planning to meet her needs when she does. Sharon's father and Named Person put forward their ideas at the Future Needs meeting and all members agree to work towards achieving this consistency.

Finding a possible solution

Jennifer's parents visit a number of schools and decide on one of them. The school rejects her application and the education authority suggests another one. Jennifer's parents are not happy with the resources offered by the alternative choice as they feel there is not enough physiotherapy input. The education authority argue that this is to be provided by the **health board** and that they are powerless to intervene. The parents approach their Named Person to ask if she will act on their behalf. She investigates and discovers that she has no legal powers but she does assist the parents in an appeal to the education authority.

Acting as a resource

Deepa's mother is deaf and uses a text telephone. Occasionally she wishes to contact the education authority or the educational psychologist quickly. Deepa's Named Person is a fluent signer and lives nearby. He is able to contact the appropriate person by phone, interpreting for Deepa's mother. The local authority does organise interpreting services for meetings but it is also helpful for Deepa's mother to have a Named Person who signs for all the general questions that may arise at any time.

Chapter 6

Action Points for Parents and Named Persons

There are many useful courses of action which parents can undertake at various points in their child's education. What follows are suggestions about a few things parents can do with the help, if necessary, of their Named Person.

1. Keeping track

If a child is thought to have special educational needs there will be regular appointments, meetings and reports.

Parents can:

- start a file of letters and papers sent and received

- keep notes of telephone calls – dates, people and conversations

- keep a diary for appointments as well as for noting who has been contacted, when and with what result

- find out the name of the officer at the education authority who answers queries and the best time for contacting him or her

- keep a note of all addresses and telephone numbers.

2. Finding out about services

Parents and Named Persons can:
- ask the Local Authority for information about special needs provision and their policies in this area

- find out what services are provided by other agencies

- do some background reading on special needs

- contact local voluntary agencies for support and information

- visit local schools and find out what they could offer.

3. Dealing with meetings

Parents will find it useful to:
- find out who will be attending any meetings, what they do and what their responsibilities are

- take someone with them to the meeting for support (this person could either be or become the Named Person). The person organising the meeting should be told beforehand if someone else is coming

- ask beforehand for copies of any papers which are to be circulated at the meeting

- before the meeting put down on paper thoughts and questions which they would like answered. It can also help to write down their own description of their child's' abilities and where they think he or she may be having difficulties. This description could be taken to the meeting and discussed, or it could be circulated to everyone involved beforehand (see Chapter 2)

- talk with others, for example the Named Person, about their views and how best to present them at meetings

- ask for an explanation of any unfamiliar words used at meetings

- ask if anyone will be producing a note of what is said at the meeting, when it will be circulated and by whom. Parents can arrange to take their own notes as well or ask the Named Person to do so

- ask the chairperson for a summary of what has been agreed at the end of the meeting. This summary should make clear who is responsible for what future action

- agree beforehand with their Named Person who should take notes and what questions each of them will ask.

4. At key moments in the Recording process

A. Assessment

If a child is to be assessed:
a) the education authority will write to parents formally explaining that their child is to be assessed. This letter will include the purpose of the assessment; the times and places of any examinations, the rights of parents to attend the medical examination; the name of the officer within the education authority who can give further advice and information

b) an educational psychologist will contact parents to arrange to see the child and will then write a report

c) if the child already attends school, his or her teacher will be asked to complete a brief report.

Parents can :
• speak to the teacher about the report

• ask for a blank copy of a Record of Needs so that they can see what information goes into it

• ask for copies of the psychologist's assessment and any other reports written about their child.

Parents will be asked to put their own views in writing about what they see as the childs' needs and how these should be met.

Parents can:
• discuss this with their Named Person and other family members

• use the profile in Chapter 2 to prepare their own report on their child.

B. If a Record of Needs is to be opened:

Parents will receive the first draft of the Record and a letter from the education authority informing them of their rights to appeal if they are unhappy with certain parts of the Record. Parents must read the draft very carefully and have 14 days to send in their comments.

Parents can :
- ask for clarification of anything that is unclear

- consider all of the reports from professionals. If any of these are inadequate, say so now

- consider what amount of **therapies** are specified (hours per week); what class size is recommended; what teaching approach is being proposed; the level of staffing; whether transport is being provided; what is being offered on the **curriculum.**

If, after consideration of the above points, parents are happy with the draft then they should simply sign it and send it back.

If parents are unhappy with the draft they can:
- discuss their unhappiness with appropriate staff (eg. the head teacher or the educational psychologist or the authority's named officer) and seek a solution to the problem.

This is important as many disagreements can be settled informally.

If parents are still unhappy once the Record is opened, however, they have 28 days once they have received a copy of the Record to make a formal appeal. The education authority will have informed parents of their rights to appeal and they can get further information from the sources in Chapter 9 (see *In special need,* Scottish Consumer Council/HMSO, 1989).

C. If a Record of Needs is not to be opened

Parents will receive a letter stating this and informing them of their rights to appeal.

If parents are happy with this decision they can:
- ask for any notes taken during the assessment to be circulated to key individuals (for example, staff at the child's school).

If parents are unhappy with this decision they can:
- consider making a formal appeal within 28 days

- ask for an extension of the 28 days if they have not received copies of all assessment reports.

D. Reviews

A child with a Record of Needs will have his or her progress reviewed regularly, both on an *informal* and a *formal* basis.

Informal reviews of all children's progress are going on all the time in school and parents should make the most of any opportunities (like parents' evenings) to keep in touch with the staff who work with their child. It is important for parents to keep staff up-to-date throughout the year with the parents' views on how their child is managing, especially if, for example, they discover new and effective ways of meeting some of their child's needs, or if they observe new and significant areas of difficulty for the child.

Many schools operate a daily home-school diary which parents can use to highlight concerns or report developments. Parents should not hesitate to contact the school at any time: there is no need to wait for a review, formal or informal.

If a child's needs do change significantly from how they were first described in the child's Record, then the education authority must conduct a *formal review* to see if the Record should be continued or changed. Parents, too, can ask for a *formal review* of the Record if one has not been held within the last 12 months, but regular parental contact as described above is welcomed by all schools.

Formal reviews are particularly useful when a child or **young person** is approaching a key stage, e.g. moving from primary to secondary school or nearing school leaving age.

What happens when there is a *formal review* is not unlike what happens when a child is first recorded. Parents will be told that a *formal review* is about to take place. Parents will have 21 days to give their views and parents can also ask for additional assessments to be carried out. They can ask for a school of their choice if a change of the school named in the Record of Needs is being suggested.

Many of the practical suggestions above about keeping track, finding out about services and dealing with meetings will also be useful to parents and to Named Persons at the *formal review* stage.

For more information about reviews, including rights of appeal for parents and young people, see *In special need,* Scottish Consumer Council (HMSO, 1989).

E. *Future Needs Assessments*

Before a child with a Record of Needs leaves school, education authorities have to carry out what is called a Future Needs Assessment. The process involved is not unlike the process of deciding to open a Record or the process of doing a formal review. In fact, Future Needs Assessment meetings are often organised as part of a formal review. Authorities usually hold at least two Future Needs Assessment meetings, the first when the child is 14+ and the second, a formal review meeting, a year or so later.

Practice varies around the country but generally what happens is that parents will be asked to attend a case conference meeting. The child or young person's teacher is usually invited, the educational psychologist, the specialist careers officer and sometimes a representative from the social work department attends (the Social Work Department is obliged by law to give its opinion on whether a child with a Record of Needs is disabled or not, with a view to assessing their needs for social work department services) and/or a representative from a further education college. It is good practice for the child or young person to be invited as well and if they have not been included parents can ask that they should be.

Parents, Named Persons and young people could find some of the practical suggestions about keeping track, coping with meetings and finding out about services helpful at this stage. Parents, Named Persons and the young person could spend some time before the meetings finding out what might be available as a next step on leaving school and talking together about their hopes and feelings for the future. The education authority must give parents and children 21 days to state their own views about future needs. Sometimes Future Needs Assessment meetings can be large and preparation can help make parents, the young person and Named Person feel more confident.

After the meeting, parents and the child or young person should receive a full note of what was decided, who is going to do what and when. The education authority has to produce a formal Future Needs Assessment report at least six months before the child or young person reaches school leaving age and it has to be sent to the parents. Before finalising this report the authority must consider parents' views and the views of children and young people. It must make a recommendation about whether a child or young person should stay on at school and about whether the Record of Needs should be continued if the child is to stay on. Copies of the report may also be sent to the health board, social work department or, with the permission of parents, to another body, such as a voluntary organisation involved with the child.

Throughout this guide the focus has been on parental involvement, parental rights and responsibilities. However, as far as possible, parents and professionals should encourage children, especially as they grow older, to be actively and confidently involved with them in discussions about their needs and the choices they face. When a child becomes a *young person* they take on certain rights of their own in relation to assessment and recording procedures.

For more information about Future Needs Assessment, who is involved and why, see *In special need,* Scottish Consumer Council (HMSO, 1989).

Chapter 7

Good Practice – Parents' Views

In the course of preparing this guide, a number of parents were asked about their experiences in the process of assessing and Recording their child. According to them the process works best when education authorities:

- make available clear and up-to-date information on their policies, procedures and resources in relation to special educational needs and on the roles of key practitioners, particularly the educational psychologist

- ensure that all correspondence and other materials are readily understood and accessible

- ensure appropriate resources for people whose first language is not English or who use alternative communication

- give ample notice of meetings, who is to be there, and ask parents if there is anyone they would like to be present

- provide parents with any report on their child in sufficient time for the content to be absorbed before the meeting and to offer them the opportunity to add issues to the agenda

- hold meetings in a way that enables the full participation of parents, bearing in mind time, location, duration and formality

- provide parents with a record of decisions made at meetings and subsequent actions agreed as soon as possible after the meeting

- promote collaborative approaches with parents and with voluntary organisations

- provide joint information and training sessions for parents, Named Persons and other practitioners

- promote a positive awareness of the needs of parents and of learners with special educational needs at all levels in the education authority

- enable key practitioners to have the time to build up and maintain good communication with, and support to, parents

- assist parents, where necessary, to identify potential Named Persons.

Parents may like to know of two publications being prepared in 1994 for the Scottish Office Education Department: a manual of *Essentials of Good Practice,* which will be for all professional staff engaged in special educational needs provision and *Effective Provision for Special Educational Needs,* a document being written by H.M. Inspectorate. In addition, the Scottish Office Education Department issued revised guidance (in draft form) in January 1994 to local authorities on assessments and recording services.

Chapter 8

Advice, Information and Support for Parents

It is not expected that the Named Person will be able to answer all of a parent's queries. Both parents and Named Persons may want to seek other sources of information and advice.

Asking someone else

The officer of the education authority (see Chapter 1), the local educational psychologist, professional staff within schools or social work departments or health board services may all be able to answer enquiries or point parents and Named Persons in the right direction.

Other individual parents who live locally or have a child with similar needs may be helpful too. Staff in schools and other services may be able to put parents in touch with others who could help.

There are also a number of voluntary agencies which provide information, advice and support to parents. Sometimes these organisations have been set up by parents and carers. Organisations may focus on a particular disability, like deafness, or on a particular group of people like single parents. Some are run entirely by volunteers but many also employ staff. There are both local and national agencies, some of which have information services, and a few offer legal advice. These services are usually free to parents and most voluntary organisations welcome enquiries. It helps if parents are as specific as possible with their questions and give some background information on their child. Some useful contacts are given in Chapter 9.

It may be useful for parents to keep a record of particularly helpful individuals and agencies for future use.

Reading material

Parents and Named Persons may also wish to do some background reading or find out about relevant publications, guides and directories. Some useful publications are listed in Chapter 9. Parents and Named Persons can also obtain from their regional council the education authority's policy on special educational needs, individual school handbooks, and directories of schools and services. These publications are usually free. Local libraries can also help with background reading and local directories of services.

Issues of confidentiality and access to information

During a child's education many reports and official records will be written by the various professional staff who come into contact with a child. Parents may have concerns about these files, particularly about who has access to these documents. They may be unclear about their rights as parents to see information held by professional staff on their child. The legal position is given below.

The Record of Needs

A copy of the Record of Needs is sent to the parent by the education authority. Parents may also ask to see a copy at the education authority offices. The Named Person, the **Secretary of State's** officials and the **Reporter** can also have access to the Record. The Named Person will not automatically be sent a copy of the Record but he or she may see a copy by asking the education authority in writing. Parents can also make a copy available to their Named Person. The Record becomes part of the **pupil's progress record** and a copy must be kept at the child's school. The education authority may disclose it to teachers, social workers, health board staff or researchers if they think it appropriate but otherwise cannot disclose its contents without the consent of the parent. Classroom teachers are not automatically given a copy but they can ask the education authority for a copy. [The Education (Record of Needs) (Scotland) Regulations 1982]

Parents can give the school written permission for anyone involved in the child's educational programme to have access to the Record of Needs.

School handbooks

The local authority must produce a school handbook for every school they manage, updated by the 15th December each year. This applies to both mainstream and special schools. The handbook must include the range of special needs the school caters for, the specialist services provided in the school, and a statement of the school's policy in relation to special educational needs.

All schools must state the number of pupils with a Record of Needs (unless the number is between 1 and 4 inclusive) and whether the school has a special class or unit. [Education (School and Placing Information) (Scotland) Regulations 1982, The Education (School and Placing Information) (Scotland) Amendment, Etc, Regulations 1993]

Access to files

Parents have a right to obtain personal information held on their child (progress records, background reports etc) subject to certain safeguards – e.g. where access to the information would endanger mental health or physical health, prejudice crime prevention, or is confidential material from a third party. Pupils also have access (if under 16 they must have parental consent). [School Pupil Records (Scotland) Regulations, 1990]

Personal information held on computer is covered by similar rules. [Data Protection Act, 1984]

Chapter 9

Further Reading and Sources of Information

For parents and Named Persons who wish to know more about special educational needs the publications listed below will provide more detailed information than can be dealt with in this guide. This is not an exhaustive list but merely a guide. A good source of advice and material for those wishing to know more about special educational needs is the local public library. If the library does not hold any item in stock then it can be ordered. The library will usually be willing to borrow material from elsewhere or buy any book if it thinks there will be enough demand for it.

The items below can be purchased or obtained from the appropriate organisation or person listed, or ordered from any good bookshop. Legislation is normally available only from HMSO bookshops.

Increasingly, education authorities are producing their own publications (guides, videos etc) on their special needs policies and provision. It is worth contacting the local education authority and asking what is available.

Publications

Contact a Family
Directory of Specific Conditions and Rare Syndromes in Children (available from Contact a Family, 170 Tottenham Court Road, London WIP 0HA Tel: 0171 383 3555) £45 plus £3 postage

Department of Education
Draft code of practice on the identification and assessment of special educational needs
(available free from DFE Publications, PO Box 2193, London E15 2EU)
This applies to England and Wales only but gives considerable detail about how parents can more effectively be involved in the assessment process. See the Scottish Office Education Department publications listed below also.

National Deaf Children's Society (1993)
The record of needs: a guide for parents of deaf children in Scotland
(available from Family Services Centre, NDCS, 24 Wakefield Road, Rothwell, Leeds LS26 0SF. Tel: 0113 2823458)
60 pages. £5.00 incl. postage. Single copies free to parents.

Royal National Institute for the Blind (1994)
Making your voice heard: a guide to assessment and the Record of Needs for visually impaired children and young people
(available from RNIB Education Centre, 10 Magdala Crescent, Edinburgh EH12 5BE. Tel: 0131 313 1876)

Russell, Philippa
The Education Act 1981 – the role of the named person
(available from Council for Disabled Children, National Children's Bureau, 8 Wakley Street, London EC1V 7QE – free with stamped addressed envelope – deals with the Named Person as defined by education law in England)

Scottish Consumer Council/HMSO (1987)
The law of the school : a parents guide to education law in Scotland
ISBN 0 11 492484 8 £5.95

Scottish Consumer Council/HMSO (1989)
In special need: a handbook for parents and young people in Scotland with special educational needs.
ISBN 0 11 493423 1 £7.50

Scottish Down's Syndrome Association
The professionals and how they can help
(available from SDSA, 158–160 Balgreen Road, Edinburgh EH11 3AU. Tel: 0131 313 4225)
20 page booklet.

Scottish Office Education Department (1989)
Provision for pupils with special educational needs – List G
A comprehensive list of all schools, special units and special classes for pupils with special educational needs.
Free

Scottish Office Education Department (1993)
A parent's guide to special educational needs
Free
This includes a useful list of organisations which assist children with special needs and their families.

Scottish Office Education Department (1993)
Information for parents in Scotland – Circular 10/93
plus
*Parents' Charter: Information for parents: Special Schools –
Circular 12/93* (amendment to Circular 10/93)
(available from SOED, Room 4/06, New St. Andrews
House, St James Centre, Edinburgh EH1 3TG. Tel: 0131
244 4902)
Details the kind of information which schools should make
available especially in school handbooks. Free

Scottish Office Education Department (January 1994)
*Children and young persons with special educational needs
(assessment and recording services) – draft circular –* guidance
to education authorities about procedures for statutory
assessment, reviews and appeals in respect of Record of
Needs. The final guidance is due out in 1995.

Stewart, Morag (1992)
Pre-school special educational needs provision – a parent's view
(available from Morag Stewart, 59 Lorne Crescent,
Monifieth, Dundee DD5 4DY – £2.00)

Stewart, Morag (1992)
*Understanding the recording process and the record of needs –
a parent's views and experiences*
(available as above – £2.00)

University of Edinburgh, Department of Education (1989)
*Policy, professionals and parents: legislating for change in the
field of special educational needs. Final report from the SED
funded project – Children with special educational needs: policy
and provision*
George O B Thomson, Sheila Riddell, Sarah Dyer.
Consultant : Jean M Lawson
(available from the Department of Education, University of
Edinburgh)

Relevant legislation and reports

These can be obtained through HMSO bookshops.

Report of the committee of enquiry into the education of handicapped children and young people. Chairman: Mrs H. M. Warnock, HMSO 1978. Cmnd 7212 £5.65 ISBN 0 10 172120 X

Education (Scotland) Act, 1980 (as amended)

Education (Record of Needs) (Scotland) Regulations, 1982 (SI 1222)

Education (Appeal Committee Procedures) (Scotland) Regulations, 1982 (SI 1736)

Education (School and Placing Information) (Scotland) Regulations, 1982 (SI 950) (as amended)

Disabled Persons (Services, Representation and Consultation) Act, 1986

Self-Governing Schools etc (Scotland) Act, 1989

School Pupil Records (Scotland) Regulations, 1990 (SI 1551)

Education (School and Placing Information) (Scotland) Amendment, Etc, Regulations, 1993

Useful organisations

There are many potential sources of advice and information, and many organisations which support parents of children with special needs. It would be impossible to list them all, especially local groups, as information and contact people change so quickly. The following organisations not only offer information and advice but can refer parents and Named Persons to other groups in their local area. For details of other useful organisations see also the SOED publication *A parents' guide to special education needs* as mentioned above.

Children in Scotland
Special Needs Forum, Princes House, 5 Shandwick Place, Edinburgh EH2 4RG
Tel : 0131 228 8484

Children in Scotland is the national agency which brings together voluntary, statutory and professional organisations and individuals to improve services and policies for Scotland's children and families. It has established a Special Needs Forum to give a higher profile to major issues affecting children and young people with disabilities or special needs and their families.
Contact the Special Needs Development Officer.

ENABLE
(formerly Scottish Society for the Mentally Handicapped)
6th Floor, 7 Buchanan Street, Glasgow G1 3HL.
Tel: 0141-226 4541

ENABLE is the main voluntary organisation in Scotland supporting children and adults with general learning disabilities and their families. It has over 70 local groups around the country and can also refer enquirers to other organisations concerned with specific learning disabilities. It provides a range of services for families including information and legal advice.
Contact the Information Service.

Disability Scotland
Princes House, 5 Shandwick Place, Edinburgh EH2 4RG
Tel: 0131 229 8632

Disability Scotland is an umbrella group. Its members are local and national disability organisations in Scotland. It welcomes enquiries from disabled people (especially those with physical disabilities) and is particularly interested in transport, access, the arts, aids and equipment, recreational facilities.
Contact the Information Department.

Contact a Family
170 Tottenham Court Road, London WIP 0HA.
Tel: 0171 383 3555

Contact a Family offers a family advisory service to all families in the UK.
Contact the Information Service.

Chapter 10

Terms Used in the Text

The following terms appear in the text. Some of these may be unfamiliar to readers so a brief explanation is given here.

assessment   a process of finding out about someone, their abilities, difficulties and needs.

case conference   a formal meeting, involving a number of professional staff, to discuss a particular individual child (or person). Each person involved with the child gives his or her view of the child's abilities and needs and often courses of action are decided.

curriculum   a list of all the different courses or learning opportunities a school offers or the particular course of study being followed by a child or young person.

education authority   an organisation legally responsible for the provision of education. In Scotland, Regional and Island authorities act as education authorities and, in practice, this duty is carried out by the education department.

educational psychologist   an educational psychologist is concerned with child development, learning and behaviour.

educational visitors
see pre-school home visiting teachers

future needs assessments
the process of finding out what a child's educational, social, training or vocational needs might be as they near the end of their school life.

health boards
are responsible for meeting all health care needs and providing services like hospitals, but also community services like GPs, physiotherapy, speech therapy, clinics.

learning difficulty
describes either a general difficulty in learning or understanding especially in comparison to people of the same age, or a specific difficulty in developing particular skills.

Named Person
the person "named" by parents on their child's Record of Needs and appointed by the education authority to support the parents with advice and information.

officer of the education authority
an employee of the education authority responsible for answering parents' enquiries on the authority's behalf.

pre-school home visiting teachers
specialist teachers who go into a child's home to work with parents in helping the child to learn and develop before he or she goes to school. Only some areas of Scotland have this service.

pupil's progress record
A record kept by the education authority for every pupil attending its schools. It contains personal information including details of progress.

Record of Needs

A legal document which details a child's special educational needs and how the education authority proposes to meet those needs. It includes space for parents' comments.

Reporter

an official of the Regional Social Work Department with a special responsibility for ensuring children's welfare. He or she is responsible for investigating cases of concern, referring cases to the local authority when appropriate, and for arranging Children's Hearings.

review

the education authority must review recorded children regularly and decide if a child's needs have changed, if the Record of Needs should be amended, or whether there continues to be a need for a Record. Parents can request a review and the authority must carry one out unless there has already been a review in the previous 12 months. Parents can also appeal against review decisions. The terms of a Future Needs Assessment report may also be reviewed.

Secretary of State (for Scotland)

the member of the Government responsible for all Scottish affairs, including education. A junior minister is usually given responsibility for education (sometimes referred to as the Minister for Education). Appeals against a Recording decision (except those to do with choice of school) are referred to the Secretary of State for decision.

social work departments

that part of the Regional authority responsible for social services, child care and adult care. They provide services to individuals and families like welfare rights advice; housing; training; holidays; supported employment; breaks for carers etc.

special educational needs

a child has special educational needs if he or she has a learning difficulty which calls for special provision to be made for him or her which is additional to or different from that generally made for children of the same age in schools managed by the education authority for the area concerned.

see also learning difficulty

therapy

teaching people to adjust or adapt to some impairment, carry out certain tasks, or to develop skills to enable them to overcome difficulties and cope with everyday life. Therapy can include physical exercise, skills training, or learning to use aids and equipment. Common therapies are physiotherapy, speech therapy, and occupational therapy.

voluntary agencies/ organisations

organisations which have been set up by people with common interests but which are not businesses, nor government agencies. The people who run these organisations "volunteer" their time and expertise although (in larger organisations especially) staff can be employed to carry out any work. It includes charities, clubs, youth organisations, campaign groups, parents self-help groups etc.

young person

in education law, a young person is someone aged over school leaving age.

Printed in Scotland for HMSO by CC No 37907 40C 11/94